DO MATH WITH SPORTS STATS!

BASEBALL

Stats, Facts, and Figures

BY KATE MIKOLEY

Gareth Stevens
PUBLISHING

Please visit our website, www.garethstevens.com. For a free color catalog of all our high-quality books, call toll free 1-800-542-2595 or fax 1-877-542-2596.

Cataloging-in-Publication Data

Names: Mikoley, Kate.
Title: Baseball: stats, facts, and figures / Kate Mikoley.
Description: New York : Gareth Stevens Publishing, 2018. | Series: Do math with sports stats! | Includes index.
Identifiers: ISBN 9781538211250 (pbk.) | ISBN 9781538211274 (library bound) | ISBN 9781538211267 (6 pack)
Subjects: LCSH: Baseball–United States–Statistics. | Baseball players–United States–Statistics. | Baseball–History–Juvenile literature. | Baseball–Juvenile literature.
Classification: LCC GV877.M55 2018 | DDC 796.357–dc23

First Edition

Published in 2018 by
Gareth Stevens Publishing
111 East 14th Street, Suite 349
New York, NY 10003

Copyright © 2018 Gareth Stevens Publishing

Designer: Samantha DeMartin
Editor: Kate Mikoley

Photo credits: pp. 4–29 (paperclips) AVS-Images/Shutterstock.com; covers, pp. 1–29 (pencil) irin-k/ Shutterstock.com; pp. 4–29 (post-its) Pixel Embargo/Shutterstock.com; pp. 4–29 (tape) Flas100/ Shutterstock.com; pp. 3–32 (graph paper) BLACKDAY/Shutterstock.com; covers, pp. 1–32 (bleacher texture) Al Sermeno Photography/Shutterstock.com; covers, pp. 1–29 (clipboard) Mega Pixel/Shutterstock.com; covers, pp. 1–29 (formula overlay) Iolya1988/Shutterstock.com; covers, pp. 1–29 (index card) photastic/ Shutterstock.com; cover, p. 1 (main) Dmytro Aksonov/E+/Getty Images; p. 5 Eric Broder Van Dyke/ Shutterstock.com; pp. 6, 13 (diagram) ugljesa/Shutterstock.com; p. 7 Gerry Boughan/Shutterstock.com; p. 8 vincent noel/Shutterstock.com; p. 9 zimmytws/Shutterstock.com; p. 10 Fort Worth Star-Telegram/ Tribune News Service/Getty Images; p. 11 Waz8/Wikimedia Commons; p. 11 (background) Image Pixel/ Shutterstock.com; p. 12 Drew Hallowell/Getty Images Sport/Getty Images; pp. 13 (top), 23 Jason Miller/ Getty Images Sport/Getty Images; p. 14 Rob Carr/Getty Images Sport/Getty Images; p. 15 (bottom) Jon Soohoo/WireImage/Getty Images; p. 15 (top) Bettmann/Bettmann/Getty Images; p. 17 Bob Levey/Getty Images Sport/Getty Images; p. 18 Mike Stobe/Getty Images Sport/Getty Images; p. 19 Frank Scherschel/ The LIFE Picture Collection/Getty Images; pp. 20, 21 (bottom) Elsa/Getty Images Sport/Getty Images; p. 21 (top) J.D. Cuban/Getty Images Sport/Getty Images; p. 21 (background) David Lee/ Shutterstock.com; p. 22 (main) Icon Sportswire/Icon Sportswire/Getty Images; p. 22 (baseballs) HP Productions/Shutterstock.com; p. 23 (background) IRIT/Shutterstock.com; p. 24 Boston Globe/ Boston Globe/Getty Images; p. 25 St. Louis Post-Dispatch/Tribune News Service/Getty Images; p. 26 eddtoro/Shutterstock.com; p. 27 New York Daily News Archive/New York Daily News/Getty Images; p. 29 Aspen Photo/Shutterstock.com.

Printed in the United States of America

CPSIA compliance information: Batch #CW18GS: For further information contact Gareth Stevens, New York, New York at 1-800-542-2595.

CONTENTS

Words in the glossary appear in **bold** type the first time they are used in the text.

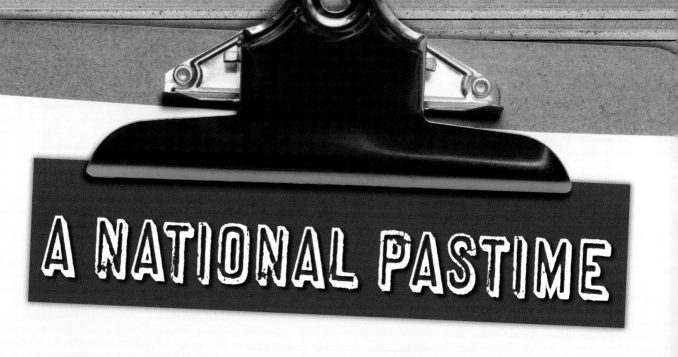

A NATIONAL PASTIME

The player steps up to the plate. He lifts the bat and readies himself for the pitch. At just the right moment, he swings. Fans watch from the stands as the ball flies across the field and over the fence. The player runs around the bases. The crowd roars as he crosses home plate.

There's a reason baseball is considered the "national **pastime**" of the United States—it's exciting! But baseball is a lot more than loud fans and home runs. Numbers and math play a large part in this popular game!

WHAT'S THAT STAT?

For more than 100 years, **statistics**, or stats, have been an important part of baseball. Stats can be used to keep track of how well an individual player does throughout a season or their entire career. Stats are also used to see how each team is doing.

GAMES SIMILAR TO BASEBALL HAVE BEEN PLAYED IN THE UNITED STATES SINCE THE 1700S. BUT IT WASN'T UNTIL 1846 THAT THE COUNTRY'S FIRST OFFICIAL GAME OF BASEBALL WAS PLAYED. TODAY, MILLIONS OF FANS ATTEND MAJOR LEAGUE BASEBALL (MLB) GAMES EVERY YEAR!

BALLPARK BASICS

No two ballparks are exactly the same. But league rules usually state that some things must be similar. In the MLB, the infield, or the part of the field enclosed by the three bases and home plate, must be a square with 90-foot (27.4 m) sides. This means each base must be 90 feet away from the bases that come before and after it.

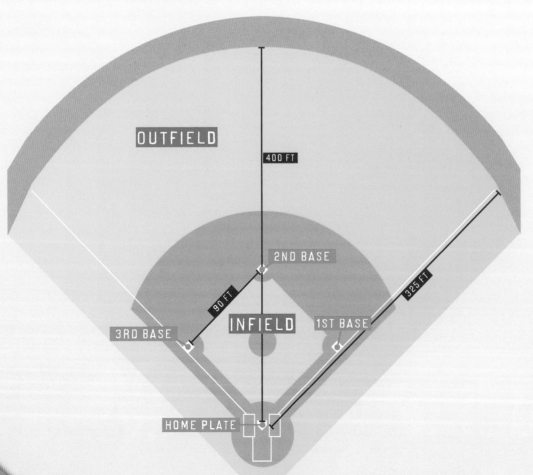

OUTFIELD

400 FT

2ND BASE

90 FT.

325 FT

INFIELD

3RD BASE

1ST BASE

HOME PLATE

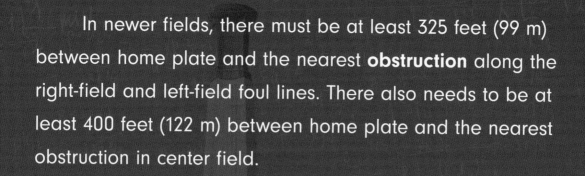

In newer fields, there must be at least 325 feet (99 m) between home plate and the nearest **obstruction** along the right-field and left-field foul lines. There also needs to be at least 400 feet (122 m) between home plate and the nearest obstruction in center field.

LOS ANGELES
MEMORIAL
COLISEUM

THE RULES ABOUT THE SIZE OF THE OUTFIELD WERE PUT IN PLACE AFTER THE DODGERS MOVED TO LOS ANGELES, CALIFORNIA IN 1958, AND PLAYED IN THE LOS ANGELES MEMORIAL COLISEUM, WHERE THE DISTANCE FROM HOME PLATE TO THE LEFT-FIELD FENCE WAS TOO SHORT.

THE NUMBERS GAME

WHEN THE BATTER MAKES A HIT, THE **PLAYER** ON THIRD BASE MUST RUN 90 FEET TO GET TO HOME **PLATE** AND SCORE A RUN. CAN YOU FIGURE OUT HOW MANY INCHES THAT **PLAYER** HAS TO MOVE TO GET THE RUN? REMEMBER, THERE ARE 12 INCHES IN 1 FOOT. ANSWER ON PAGE 29.

WHAT'S IN AN INNING?

Most baseball games have nine innings. Innings are divided into two halves, called the "top" and "bottom." The top of the inning is the part in which the first team, usually the visiting team, is batting. The bottom is when the second team, usually the home team, is batting. Each team gets three outs per inning. That's six total outs per inning.

The line score, often shown on scoreboards, shows each team's progress per inning. The number of runs each team scores per inning is shown on the line score.

	1	2	3	4	5	6	7	8	9	10	R	H	E
VISITOR	0	0	0	0	0						0	3	0
HOME	2	0	0	0							2	6	0

BALLS   STRIKES   OUTS   H   E

THE NUMBERS GAME

A DOUBLEHEADER IS WHEN TWO TEAMS PLAY EACH OTHER TWICE IN A ROW ON THE SAME DAY.

AFTER A DOUBLEHEADER, THE HOME TEAM HAS MADE A TOTAL OF 18 RUNS. ONE-THIRD OF THESE RUNS WERE SCORED IN THE FIRST GAME. HOW MANY RUNS WERE SCORED IN THE SECOND GAME? ANSWER ON PAGE 29.

Hint. $18 \times \dfrac{1}{3} =$ *number of runs in the first game*

Most baseball games have nine innings, but some end before the full nine innings are played. They may get shortened for rain or other unsafe conditions. As long as five innings have been completed, it's considered a **regulation game**. The game counts, and whichever team is in the lead wins.

An umpire calls the game due to rain!

Games can also be more than nine innings if the game is tied at the end of the ninth inning. The longest game in organized baseball history happened in 1981 when the Pawtucket Red Sox and Rochester Red Wings played a game that lasted 33 innings!

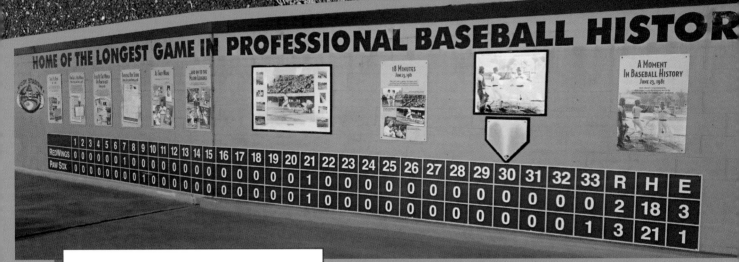

HOME OF THE LONGEST GAME IN PROFESSIONAL BASEBALL HISTORY

	1	2	3	4	5	6	7	8	9	10	11	12	13	14	15	16	17	18	19	20	21	22	23	24	25	26	27	28	29	30	31	32	33	R	H	E
REDWINGS	0	0	0	0	0	0	1	0	0	0	0	0	0	0	0	0	0	0	0	0	1	0	0	0	0	0	0	0	0	0	0	0	0	2	18	3
PAW SOX	0	0	0	0	0	0	0	1	0	0	0	0	0	0	0	0	0	0	0	0	1	0	0	0	0	0	0	0	0	0	0	0	1	3	21	1

THE LONGEST GAME HAPPENED AT MCCOY STADIUM IN PAWTUCKET, RHODE ISLAND.

The line score for the longest game

THE NUMBERS GAME

LET'S SAY A GAME IS TIED AT THE END OF THE NINTH INNING. THE TEAMS COMPLETE THREE MORE INNINGS, BUT NEITHER TEAM GETS ANOTHER RUN. HOW MANY OUTS HAVE THERE BEEN TOTAL SO FAR? REMEMBER, THERE ARE SIX OUTS PER INNING. ANSWER ON PAGE 29.

$$(9 + 3) \times 6$$

KNOW YOUR POSITION

Every player on a team has an important role. If a team is up to bat, they're playing offense. This means they're trying to score. When the team is out on the field, they're playing defense, or trying to prevent the other team from scoring.

When playing defense, a team has nine positions to fill. Of these nine positions, there are three outfielders. They play right field, center field, and left field. The other players generally stay closer to the infield. They include the pitcher, catcher, first baseman, second baseman, shortstop, and third baseman.

Troy Tulowitzki playing offense

THE NUMBERS GAME

MOST TEAMS HAVE AN ACTIVE **ROSTER** OF 25 PLAYERS. THESE ARE THE 25 PLAYERS THAT NORMALLY TRAVEL WITH THE TEAM AND PLAY IN THE GAMES. CAN YOU FIGURE OUT HOW MANY FACTORS OF 25 THERE ARE? WHAT ARE THEY? REMEMBER, FACTORS ARE NUMBERS YOU CAN MULTIPLY TOGETHER TO GET ANOTHER NUMBER. ANSWER ON PAGE 29.

THE SHORTSTOP AND SECOND BASEMAN NEED TO WORK TOGETHER. THEY BOTH HAVE TO COVER SECOND BASE SOMETIMES, DEPENDING ON WHERE THE BALL IS.

Jason Kipnis (second baseman)
and Francisco Lindor (shortstop)
of the Cleveland Indians

CENTER FIELDER

LEFT FIELDER

RIGHT FIELDER

SECOND BASEMAN

SHORTSTOP

PITCHER

THIRD BASEMAN

FIRST BASEMAN

CATCHER

PLAYERS MOVE ALL OVER THE FIELD, DEPENDING ON WHAT HAPPENS AND WHERE THE BALL GOES. THIS SHOWS THE GENERAL AREA WHERE MOST OF THE ACTION TAKES PLACE FOR EACH POSITION.

HEY, BATTER!

Since the object of the game is to score more runs than the other team, some would say runs are an important stat in baseball. A player gets a run if they safely pass first, second, and third base and return to home plate.

A stat called runs batted in (RBI) measures the total number of runs that a batter has helped make happen. If a player makes a hit, they may only get on first base. But if another player makes it to home plate because of that hit, it usually counts as an RBI for that batter. The player that crossed home plate gets a run.

HIT IT HOME

Most of the time, the player who gets the RBI isn't the one who crosses home plate and gets the run. But sometimes they are! If a player hits a home run, that counts as both a run and an RBI for them.

Bryce Harper crosses home plate.

HANK AARON HOLDS THE RECORD FOR MOST CAREER RBIs OF ANY MAJOR LEAGUE BASEBALL PLAYER, WITH 2,297. BUT THE PLAYER WITH THE MOST RUNS IN THEIR CAREER IS RICKEY HENDERSON, WITH 2,295 RUNS!

Hank Aaron

Rickey Henderson

GET SOME HITS

Each time a player goes up to bat, it's called a plate appearance. Three things can happen in a plate appearance: a walk, a hit, or an out. If the batter gets a hit or an out, it's also counted as an "at bat."

In baseball, a hit is when a player bats the ball in play and safely reaches base. An out is either when a player strikes out, their ball is caught, or they're thrown out before reaching a base. A player's batting average is the total number of hits a player has divided by their number of at bats.

THE NUMBERS GAME

IN THE 2016 SEASON, OUTFIELDER MIKE TROUT PLAYED 159 GAMES WITH THE LOS ANGELES ANGELS. TROUT HAD 173 HITS IN 549 AT BATS. THAT'S A .315 BATTING AVERAGE!

IF TROUT PLAYED 25 GAMES AND HAD 20 HITS IN 100 AT BATS, WHAT'S HIS BATTING AVERAGE? ANSWER ON PAGE 29.

$$\frac{20 \text{ hits}}{100 \text{ at bats}}$$

MANY BASEBALL FANS THINK BATTING .300 IS ONE MARK OF A GOOD PLAYER. OTHERS THINK OTHER STATS ARE MORE IMPORTANT BECAUSE THE STAT DOESN'T INCLUDE WALKS!

Mike Trout

If a pitcher throws four pitches outside the **strike zone** and the hitter doesn't swing at any, the hitter gets to move to first base. This is called a walk. Sometimes a pitcher will purposely walk a good hitter to avoid giving them a chance to get a hit and maybe get a home run.

A player's on-base percentage (OBP) refers to how often they get on base, or don't get an out. This includes walks, hits, and **hit-by-pitches**. A player's **approximate** OBP is figured out by dividing the number of times they get on base by the total number of plate appearances they have.

Anthony Rizzo gets hit by a pitch.

THE NUMBERS GAME

A PLAYER'S OBP IS USUALLY SHOWN AS A DECIMAL, BUT IT COULD ALSO BE SHOWN AS A FRACTION.

CAN YOU FIGURE OUT THE FRACTION THAT WOULD REPRESENT THE OBP OF A PLAYER WITH THE STATS BELOW? ANSWER ON PAGE 29.

walks: 14 hits: 23
hit-by-pitches: 1 plate appearances: 100

TED WILLIAMS HOLDS THE RECORD FOR BEST CAREER OBP IN THE MLB, AT 0.4817, THOUGH MANY WOULD CONSIDER ANYTHING OVER 0.370 TO BE A GREAT OBP.

LET'S PITCH!

Some people say the pitcher is the most important player in the game. The pitcher starts every play by throwing the ball to home plate. They're responsible for when a batter gets a walk, but they're also the reason a player might strike out.

One of the best measures of a pitcher's performance is their Earned Run Average (ERA). This represents the number of runs scored on a pitcher for every nine innings they've pitched. To find this number, you divide their earned runs by the number of innings they've pitched and multiply that number by 9.

Dellin Betances pitches the ball.

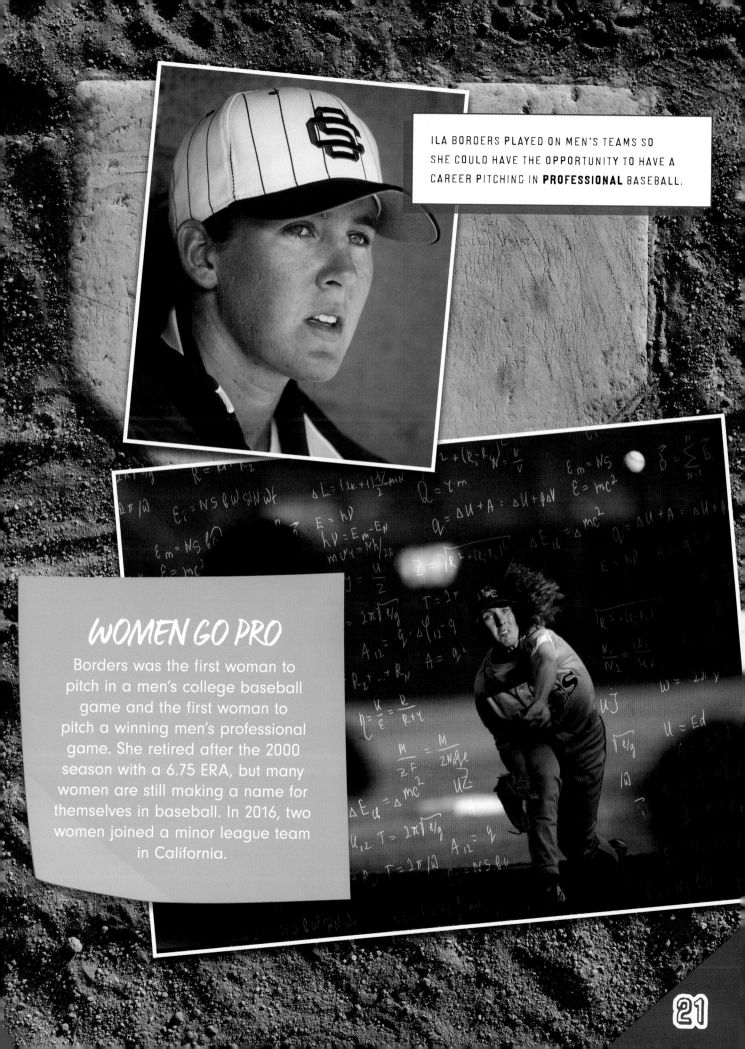

ILA BORDERS PLAYED ON MEN'S TEAMS SO SHE COULD HAVE THE OPPORTUNITY TO HAVE A CAREER PITCHING IN **PROFESSIONAL** BASEBALL.

WOMEN GO PRO

Borders was the first woman to pitch in a men's college baseball game and the first woman to pitch a winning men's professional game. She retired after the 2000 season with a 6.75 ERA, but many women are still making a name for themselves in baseball. In 2016, two women joined a minor league team in California.

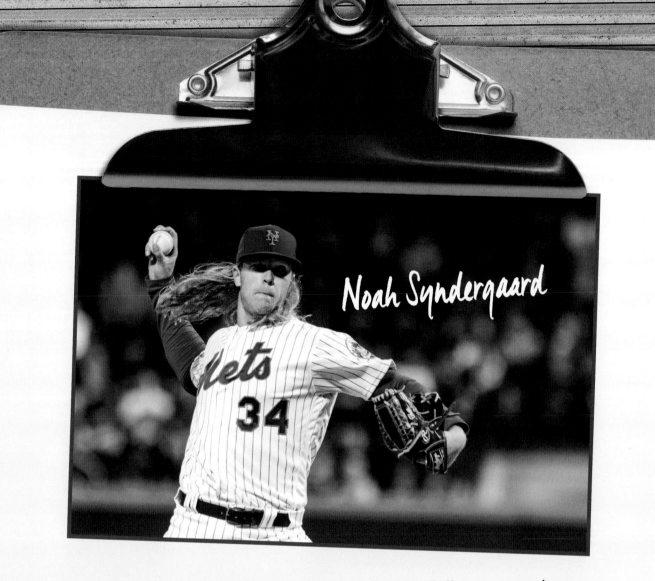

Noah Syndergaard

Another way to measure a pitcher's skill is to see how well they keep the hitters off the bases. This can be measured with Walks and Hits per Inning Pitched (WHIP). To figure out a pitcher's WHIP, you first add the number of walks and hits that have occurred while they were pitching. You then divide that number by the total innings they have pitched.

One thing WHIP doesn't reflect is how the hitter got to base. For example, a home run is usually more harmful for a pitcher than a walk, but WHIP doesn't show this.

WER THE WHIP, THE
R THE PITCHER PROBABLY
2016, CLAYTON KERSHAW
ED 149 INNINGS WITH THE
NGELES DODGERS AND HAD A
OF 0.72!

THE NUMBERS GAME

THE MORE INNINGS PITCHED, THE MORE ACCURATE A PLAYER'S WHIP WIL

PROBABLY BE. A PLAYER COULD PITCH ONLY 3 INNINGS AND HAVE A GREA

WHIP, BUT PITCHING MORE INNINGS WILL SHOW IF THEY'RE **CONSISTENT.**

IF A PITCHER PITCHED FOR 30 INNINGS AND THREW 46 HITS AND 14 WALK

WHAT'S THEIR WHIP? ANSWER ON PAGE 29.

$$(46 + 14) \div 30$$

DON'T MAKE AN ERROR

Stats are kept for poor play, too. A fielder who makes a mistake gets an error. Errors happen lots of ways. As a general rule, a fielder gets an error if they make a mistake that prevents an out that would have otherwise probably happened. Errors are often considered an important stat for defenders. Players with fewer errors are often considered better defenders than players with more errors.

Collisions can cause errors!

THE NUMBERS GAME

SOME BATTERS GET THOUSANDS OF RBIs IN THEIR CAREER.
LET'S SAY A PLAYER BATTED IN 2,107 RUNS, INCLUDING ALL THE ONES THAT
HAPPENED BECAUSE OF ERRORS. IT TURNS OUT 46 OF THESE HAPPENED
BECAUSE OF ERRORS MADE BY FIELDERS. HOW MANY RBIs DOES THE
PLAYER HAVE? ANSWER ON PAGE 29.

IF A FIELDER DROPS A
BALL THEY COULD EASILY
HAVE CAUGHT, THEY WILL
PROBABLY GET AN ERROR.

Errors don't only affect the fielder. They also affect other stats.
For example, any runs that wouldn't have happened if there hadn't
been an error don't count toward a batter's RBI.

TEAM STATS

While stats are especially important for individuals, the combined stats of each player on a team matter, too. Team stats show how teams stack up to one another. A team can have the best player in the league, but if the rest of the team doesn't also do well, the team probably won't win many games.

THE CHAMPIONSHIPS

The World Series is the championship series of the MLB. Teams from the two major leagues, the American League and the National League, compete for the winning title. Since the series was first played in 1903, the New York Yankees have won the most World Series titles of any MLB team.

Team stats can also help **predict** which teams will likely do well in the **postseason** and make it to the championship games. The teams with the best win-loss records usually get the chance to move forward and play in a series of games to become the winner of the overall season.

BEATING THE STATS

Numbers and stats are such an important part of baseball that the records are always changing. But records in baseball can be a tough topic because some of the players who hold them have been known to use **steroids**. Still, many players work hard to break records fairly. A record that's been held for 100 years could be broken tomorrow!

Many of the best players get **inducted** into the National Baseball Hall of Fame, located in Cooperstown, New York. The Hall of Fame showcases many of the best players, umpires, and managers in baseball. Many players with the best stats get honored there every year!

A TOURIST DESTINATION

The National Baseball Hall of Fame and Museum is a popular place for baseball fans to visit. Around 300,000 people make the trip to Cooperstown every year to learn about the hundreds of people inducted in the Hall of Fame since it opened in 1939.

ANSWER KEY

p. 7 – 1080 inches

p. 9 – 12 runs

p. 11 – 72 outs

p. 12 – 3 factors: 1, 5, 25

p. 16 – .200 batting average

p. 19 – $\frac{38}{100}$ (simplified $\frac{19}{50}$)

p. 23 – 2.0 WHIP

p. 25 – 2,061 RBI

THE NATIONAL BASEBALL HALL OF FAME AND MUSEUM FEATURES EXHIBITS ON THE HISTORY OF BASEBALL AND THE MANY PEOPLE WHO HAVE CONTRIBUTED TO IT.

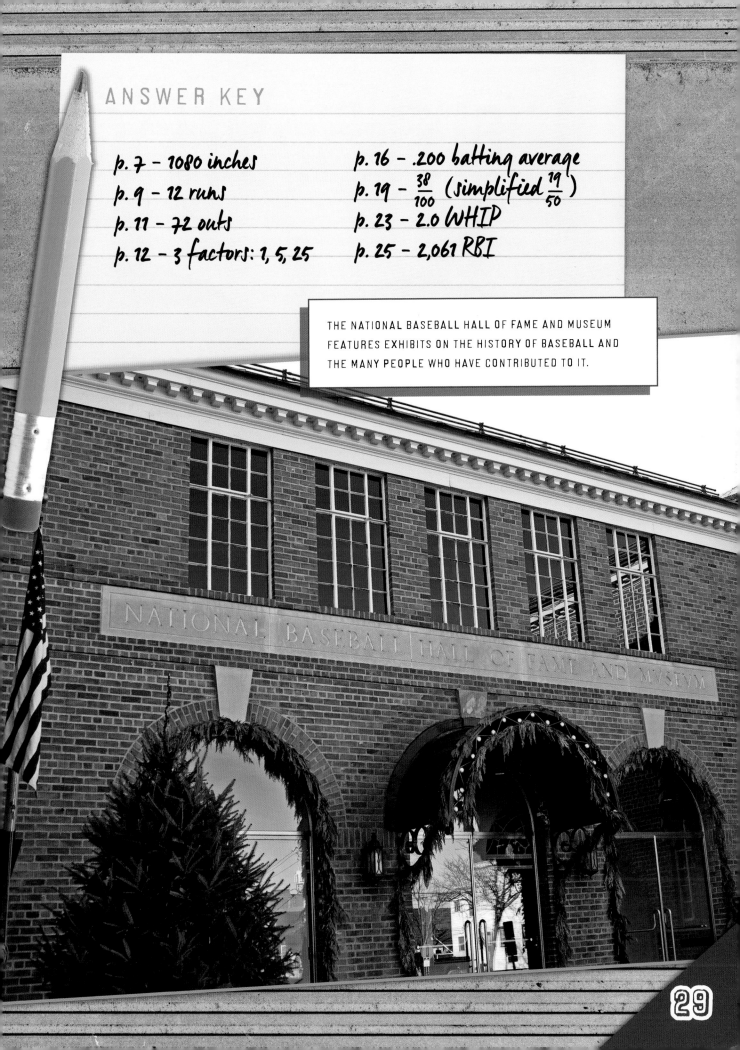

GLOSSARY

approximate: almost correct or exact

consistent: always acting or performing the same way

hit-by-pitch: a situation when a batter or their clothing or equipment is hit by a pitch

induct: to officially include someone in a group or organization, such as the Hall of Fame

obstruction: something that blocks something else

pastime: an activity that someone enjoys during their free time

postseason: games played after the regular season

predict: to guess what will happen in the future based on facts or knowledge

professional: earning money from an activity that many people do for fun

regulation game: an official game that is considered complete, even if the full nine innings aren't played

roster: the list of people that are on a team

statistics: information that can be related in numbers

steroids: a drug that is sometimes used illegally by athletes to help them become stronger or do better at their sport

strike zone: the imaginary rectangular area over the plate between the batter's knees and armpits that is the pitcher's target

FOR MORE INFORMATION

BOOKS

Braun, Eric. *Baseball Stats and the Stories Behind Them: What Every Fan Needs to Know.* North Mankato, MN: Capstone Press, 2016.

Graubart, Norman D. *The Science of Baseball.* New York, NY: PowerKids Press, 2016.

Murray, Stuart. *Score with Baseball Math.* Berkeley Heights, NJ: Enslow Publishers, 2014.

WEBSITES

Baseball: Statistics
www.ducksters.com/sports/baseball/statistics.php
Read more about the basics of baseball stats on this webpage.

Standard Stats
m.mlb.com/glossary/standard-stats
Learn about specific stats and watch videos of examples from the official MLB website.

INDEX